Fulton Books, Inc.
Meadville, PA

Published by Fulton Books 2021

ISBN 978-1-63860-947-6 (paperback)
ISBN 978-1-64952-871-1 (hardcover)
ISBN 978-1-64952-870-4 (digital)

Printed in the United States of America

Photo Credit: Jordan Fernandes

About the Authors

Barry and Dari Anne Amato have been married for twenty-four years and reside in Nashville, Tennessee, with their sheepadoodle, Dorothy. The two met as singers/dancers at the former theme park Opryland USA in Nashville. Together, the two own and operate their own entertainment production company, Paws-itive Productions. Their careers have spanned nearly thirty years producing television, both on and off camera, and live entertainment along with being professional emcees and choreographers for corporate events, theme parks, and pageants. Following their years as producers and segment hosts for an internationally syndicated dance television show out of Nashville, the pair traveled globally as instructors/choreographers. Timmy and the FurTastics is dedicated to the memory of their golden retriever, Timmy, who was their heart dog for eight years. Their hope is that this book will be a lasting legacy and an inspiration to children through his story.

Timmy and the FURTASTICS

Barry and Dari Anne Amato

Illustrated by Dari Anne Amato

I love to chase tennis balls and butterflies
and roll in clover and take long naps.

My friend Jimmy is our paperboy.

Every morning he scratches my head and gives me the newspaper.

I'm gonna learn lots of new things and make loads of new friends.

Hey, I'm Cowboy, don't pay not mind to those FUR BALLS. They're all the same. You and me though, we're different. Come on, partner, let's be pals.

I knew I'd make a friend today. Hey Cowboy, you said we are different. What's different about me?

Well Timmy, you only have three legs and the cool cats and poodles have four legs.

I'm Timmy. I have three legs, and I love to run.

I'm Cowboy. I don't have a tail, and when I'm happy, my butt wiggles.

I'm Harriett. I can't see through my bangs, but I know who my friends are.

I'm Tank. I'm the smallest on the playground, but I have the biggest heart.

I'm Patch. I only have one eye, but I can always sniff my way to the cookie jar.

We're all different, but together we're furtastic!

SPRING, SUMMER, WINTER, FALL FURTASTICS ARE THE BEST OF ALL!

CPSIA information can be obtained
at www.ICGtesting.com
Printed in the USA
BVRC101103011121
620447BV00003B/71